HER RUCK

Inside The Emotional Backpack
of Military Wives

By Richelle Futch, MSW

ISBN-13: 978-1721936779
ISBN-10: 1721936777

CONTENTS..

HER RUCK

In the military, service members carry a ruck·sack or ruck. It is essentially a large backpack where they store their gear when they need to move from one location to another. These packs typically range from 25lbs to 75lbs depending on what is on their packing list, and the weapons they carry. During training, these service members pack their rucks and do marches anywhere from 3-10 miles on average.

As you can imagine, walking 10 miles in formation could be difficult on it's own, now add 35 or 60 lbs to that and it gets even tougher. We know that our service members carry a lot more than gear on their shoulders. They also carry family stress, responsibilities, war injuries, and mental health issues.

This work-book is not about the things they carry, this is about the things WE carry because we love them and chose the military spouse life. This is about what is in OUR Ruck.

This workbook will address not only our stress and our responsibilities, but will offer solutions to build a better relationship with yourself, your children, and your spouse while also giving you new skills to navigate all the surprises, disappointments, and crisis that comes with the military life.

HER RUCK

THE WEIGHT WE CARRY

Let's face it, being a military spouse brings forth a lot of exciting and stressful issues and events not found with our civilian counterparts. Sure, we get married, and they get married. We move and they move, but it is not the same.

Let's list as many stressors (positive & negative) that we deal with as military spouses. Create a list below.

....

....

....

....

....

....

....

....

....

....

....

....

SHARE WITH THE GROUP
or if completing individually
check out our list at www.herruck.com

Worksheets | 5

HER RUCK

HOW DO WE EXPRESS OUR STRESS

Changing jobs, dealing with a separation from your spouse, moving, struggling financially are some of the most common stressors amongst military families. Since these occurrences are so prevalent, many of us assume we shouldn't feel stress or aren't allowed to express stress in relation to these events.

This means you may be walking around with way more stress than you realize, and probably aren't appropriately dealing with it.

Some of the signs you may be experiencing more stress than you realize include: A change in sleep pattern, decline in health, your body is sending you hints (ie frequent headaches or stomach aches, irregular bowel movements), you've lost interest in your favorite things, you are not keeping up your normal standard of appearance, your moods are limited to angry or sad, your eating habits have changed, you constantly feel tired, you are using bad habits to deal with your stress (drinking/smoking), you feel alone but do not want to go out.

What does it look like when you experience stress?

....

....

....

....

SHARE WITH THE GROUP
or if completing individually
check out our list at www.herruck.com

HER RUCK

Your Emotional Backpack

"It's not the load that breaks you down, it's the way you carry it."

– Lou Holtz

Every day we wake up and start our day wearing an invisible backpack. This backpack is filled with long term and short term vulnerabilities, events (good and bad) , conversations, and everything else we deal with during our day or the days prior sometimes years prior) . Some people have amazing protective factors! For them, their pack doesn't seem so heavy. They go about their day and accomplish things, smile, and volunteer at the FRG (just kidding). For others, the weight is so heavy, they may isolate, experience anxiety, depression, and other factors.

Getting a clear picture of your stress level is important. It helps raise awareness to yourself. If you confide in your family it helps them adjust to accommodate your needs. One of the most commonly used stress inventories is the Holmes - Rahe Life Stress Inventory. Take the inventory on the next page.

Of the 125 military spouses surveyed, major changes in living conditions, changes in sleep patterns, changes in eating patterns, and changes in frequency of arguments with their spouse were noted by more than 50% of the wives.

The Holmes-Rahe Life Stress Inventory
The Social Readjustment Rating Scale
INSTRUCTIONS: Mark down the point value of each of these life events that has happened to you during the previous year. Total these associated points.

Life Event	Mean Value
1. Death of spouse	100
2. Divorce	73
3. Marital Separation from mate	65
4. Detention in jail or other institution	63
5. Death of a close family member	63
6. Major personal injury or illness	53
7. Marriage	50
8. Being fired at work	47
9. Marital reconciliation with mate	45
10. Retirement from work	45
11. Major change in the health or behavior of a family member	44
12. Pregnancy	40
13. Sexual Difficulties	39
14. Gaining a new family member (i.e.. birth, adoption, older adult moving in, etc)	39
15. Major business readjustment	39
16. Major change in financial state (i.e.. a lot worse or better off than usual)	38
17. Death of a close friend	37
18. Changing to a different line of work	36
19. Major change in the number of arguments w/spouse (i.e.. either a lot more or a lot less than usual regarding child rearing, personal habits, etc.)	35
20. Taking on a mortgage (for home, business, etc..)	31
21. Foreclosure on a mortgage or loan	30
22. Major change in responsibilities at work (i.e. promotion, demotion, etc.)	29
23. Son or daughter leaving home (marriage, attending college, joined mil.)	29
24. In-law troubles	29
25. Outstanding personal achievement	28
26. Spouse beginning or ceasing work outside the home	26
27. Beginning or ceasing formal schooling	26
28. Major change in living condition (new home, remodeling, deterioration of neighborhood or home etc.)	25
29. Revision of personal habits (dress manners, associations, quitting smoking)	24
30. Troubles with the boss	23
31. Major changes in working hours or conditions	20
32. Changes in residence	20
33. Changing to a new school	20
34. Major change in usual type and/or amount of recreation	19
35. Major change in church activity (i.e.. a lot more or less than usual)	19
36. Major change in social activities (clubs, movies, visiting, etc.)	18
37. Taking on a loan (car, tv, freezer, etc)	17
38. Major change in sleeping habits (a lot more or a lot less than usual)	16
39. Major change in number of family get-togethers ("")	15
40. Major change in eating habits (a lot more or less food intake, or very different meal hours or surroundings)	15
41. Vacation	13
42. Major holidays	12
43. Minor violations of the law (traffic tickets, jaywalking, disturbing the peace, etc)	11

Now, add up all the points you have to find your score.

150pts or less means a relatively low amount of life change and a low susceptibility to stress-induced health breakdown.

150 to 300 pts implies about a 50% chance of a major health breakdown in the next 2 years.

300pts or more raises the odds to about 80%, according to the Holmes-Rahe statistical prediction model.

HER RUCK

DISCOVERING THE CONTENTS OF YOUR BACKPACK

Let's face it, being a military spouse brings forth a lot of exciting and stressful issues and events not found with our civilian counterparts. Sure, we get married, and they get married. We move and they move, but it is not the same.

What is your initial response to your score?

....

....

What is something you feel is not covered or accurately captured in the inventory?

....

....

....

It isn't enough to just identify your stress. We want to find healthy ways of coping and dealing with our stress. Our support system is so important. Who can you share these results with?

....

....

....

LEARN MORE ABOUT
Vulnerabilities on our website at www.herruck.com

STRESS VS. VULNERABILITIES

Vulnerability refers to our basic susceptibility to mental health disorders. This is determined by our genetic makeup and our early life experiences. Stress refers to the challenges faced in our lives. It is affected by our coping skills, social support, and involvement in meaningful activities.

Look at the figure below. It represents how stress and vulnerabilities contribute to mental health symptoms.

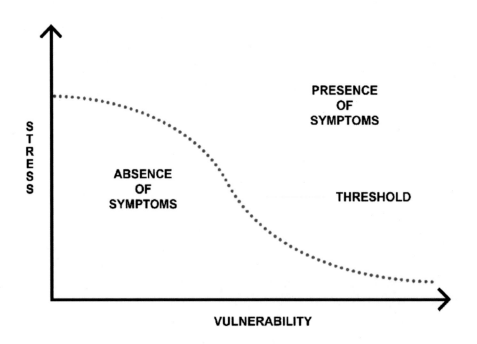

Biological Vulnerabilities + Stress = Mental Illness

LEARN MORE ABOUT

Vulnerabilities on our website at www.herruck.com

Vulnerability Vs Stress Cont...

Here are some examples of how Biological Vulnerability & Stress impact you.

You may feel more vulnerable at night to someone breaking into your home when your husband is deployed. The stress is your husband is not home, the biological vulnerability is that as a woman, you may not feel as strong to fight off a male intruder.

You may feel more vulnerable while pregnant and walking to your car alone.

Stress = fear of being mugged
Biological Vulnerability = pregnant

You may feel more vulnerable to having a short temper with your family the day you are starting a new job.

Stress = New Job
Biological Vulnerability = low tolerance to frustration.

Take a moment and list a few of your current biological vulnerabilities and stressors: <They can be short term ie: feel sick or long term ie: being sexually assaulted at age 15. > *This does not need to be shared.

LEARN MORE ABOUT
Stress on our website at www.herruck.com

HER RUCK

Reviewing the following terms will help us get a clear picture for the skills we are going to learn later in this workbook.

Risk Factors are conditions or variables associated with a lower likelihood of positive outcomes and a higher likelihood of negative or socially undesirable outcomes. For example: Smoking cigarettes is a risk factor for getting lung cancer.

Protective factors are conditions and variables which decrease the likelihood of negative or socially undesirable outcomes and increase the likelihood of positive outcomes. For example: Taking a parenting class before having children.

Resiliency is the ability of individuals to remain healthy even in the presence of risk factors. To recover quickly from difficulties

Prevention is stopping something before it arises. We do this for our health by going to the doctor for check-ups, counseling, brushing our teeth, etc.

LEARN MORE ABOUT
these definitions on our website at www.herruck.com

HER RUCK

MORE ON PROTECTIVE FACTORS

Protective factors are conditions or attributes (skills, strengths, resources, supports or coping strategies) in individuals, families, communities or the larger society that help people deal more effectively with stressful events and mitigate or eliminate risk in families and communities.

Examples of Protective Factors include: Personal Resilience, Social Connectedness, Concrete Support In Times of Need, Knowledge & Understanding, and Positive Personality Traits.

Imagine you just received a text: Your husband has to deploy for 10 months in 6 days. (*Alternative scenarios:* 1. Imagine your elderly parent just got hurt and can no longer live independently. 2. Imagine you're just found a lump on your breast. 3. Create your own possible stressful scenario:)

List the protective factors you have to cope with the stress.

....

....

....

....

....

....

....

LEARN MORE ABOUT
Protective Factors on our website at www.herruck.com

HER RUCK

WHAT IS MINDFULNESS

Mindfulness is a mental state achieved by focusing one's awareness on the present moment while calmly acknowledging and accepting one's feelings, thoughts, and bodily sensations.

Research shows that mindfulness training can effectively protect against the decline of executive functions (i.e., attention, working memory) and benefit psychological well-being over high-demand intervals.

Being Mindful takes practice. There are 2 types of Mindfulness Practice that helps to increase staying in the present and raising awareness to your thoughts, feelings, and body sensations in the moment.

1. Focus Mindfulness and
2. Activity Mindfulness.

Focusing Mindfulness Practices are exercises where you are instructed or guided on what to focus, ie: breathing, meditation, imagery, specific thoughts. The goal of this is to recognize drifting thoughts, judgments, and body sensations.

Activity Mindfulness Practices are exercises where you are participating in an activity ie: throwing a ball, memory games, and sports. The goal of this is to participate fully without judgement, and complete awareness of the activity.

LOOK FOR

Mindfulness Activities on our website at www.herruck.com

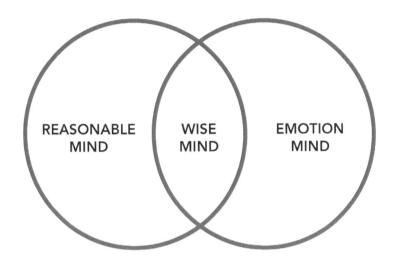

Reasonable Mind is cool, rational, task-focused. When in reasonable mind, you are ruled by facts, reason, logic, and pragmatics. Values and feelings are not important.

Wise Mind is the wisdom within each person. It is seeing the value of both reason and emotion. Bringing the left and right brain together. The middle path.

Emotion Mind is hot, mood-dependent, and emotion focused. When in emotion mind, you are ruled by your moods, feelings, and urges to do or say things. Facts, reason, and logic are not important.

LEARN MORE ABOUT

the 3 States of Mind on our website www.herruck.com

HER RUCK

THE 3 STATES OF MIND ACTIVITY

What does it look and feel like when you are in Reasonable Mind? What activities might be more effective while in Reasonable Mind?

....

....

....

....

What does it look and feel like when you are in Wise Mind? What activities might be more effective while in Wise Mind?

....

....

....

....

What does it look and feel like when you are in Emotion Mind? What activities might be more effective while in Emotion Mind?

....

....

....

....

LEARN MORE ABOUT

3 States of Mind on our website www.herruck.com

HER RUCK

TAKING HOLD OF YOUR MIND

What should you be doing to be Mindful?

Observing: Notice your body sensations, Pay Attention on purpose, Control your attention, practice wordless watching, observe both inside and outside of yourself.

Describing: Put words on the experience, label what you observe, unglue your interpretations and opinions from the facts, remember, if you can't observe it through your senses, you can't describe it.

Participating: Throw yourself completely into activities of the current moment. Become one with whatever you are doing completely forgetting about yourself. Acti intuitively from wise mind by doing just what is needed in each situation. Go with the flow.

How do you do this?

Non-judgmentally: See, but don't evaluate as good or bad. Just stick to the facts. Accept each moment. Acknowledge the difference between the helpful and the harmful, the safe and the dangerous, but don't judge them.

One-Mindfully: Be completely present to this one moment. Do one thing at a time. Notice the desire to be half-present to be somewhere else, when you are eating, eat. When you are walking, walk.

Effectively: Be mindful of your goals in the situation, and do what is necessary to achieve them. Focus on what works, Play by the rules.

LEARN MORE ABOUT

Taking hold of your mind at www.herruck.com

HER RUCK

Often times our effectiveness is clouded by our judgments. When we judge ourselves as right or justified, we can lose sight of what is needed to be done to be effective. Our goals get lost by digging our heals into being right.

We see this happen in our personal relationships. Think of a time when you were in a discussion with your spouse about something that needed to be done and you argued about who should do it, how it should be done, or when it should be done.

While either of you 'telling' the other to do something may or may not be effective at getting the task done, it probably isn't effective at maintaining a positive relationship while getting the task done.

Remember it is more important to be effective than it is to be right.

There are usually 3 things always at play in any situation. The objective you want met, the relationship with the person involved, and the relationship with yourself (self respect).

LEARN MORE ABOUT

Vulnerabilities on our website at www.herruck.com

HER RUCK

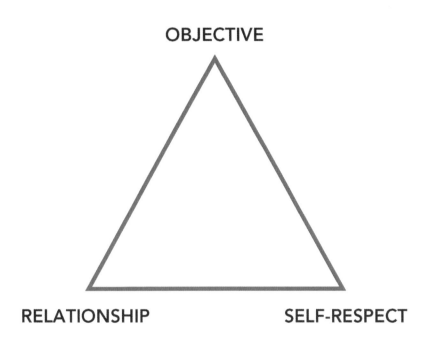

OBJECTIVE

RELATIONSHIP   SELF-RESPECT

The objective, relationship, and your self-respect is represented above on a triangle because they are all of equal importance. During every interaction however, the priority of importance changes. Sometimes you absolutely MUST get your objective met and other times you feel you must put the relationship or yourself respect first.

Note: If you are always putting the relationship first, you will feel like a pushover, people pleaser, and your self-respect will suffer. If you always put yourself first, your relationships with others will suffer. It is important to recognize a balance in every situation.

CONTINUE LEARNING ABOUT

Objective Effectiveness at www.herruck.com

HER RUCK

OBJECTIVE

Priority ....

RELATIONSHIP
Priority ....

SELF-RESPECT
Priority ....

Step 1: Define Your Objective: ....

Step 2: Describe How You Want To Feel About The Relationship With The Other Person At The End Of The Interaction:

....

Step 3: Describe How You Want To Feel About Yourself At The End Of The Interaction ....

Step 4: On the lines beside the triangle Number 1-3 the priority of importance in this one situation (often times people want to always put the relationship with their spouse or child first thinking they are the most important, but remember not in EVERY daily situation do you need to place them #1. We know they are #1 overall in your life.

LOOK FOR

an example at www.herruck.com

HER RUCK

WHAT TO DO WHEN YOUR OBJECTIVE IS # 1

If your OBJECTIVE is your top priority, than use the DEARMAN skill.

(D) Describe the current situation. Stick to the facts.

(E) Express your feelings and opinions about the situation.

(A) Assert yourself by asking for what you want.

(R) Reinforce (reward) the person ahead of time by explaining positive effects of getting what you want.

(M) stay MINDFUL and keep your focus on your goals.

(A) Appear Confident in tone and body language.

(N) Negotiate. Be willing to give to get. Offer and ask for other solutions to the problem.

Remember to be brief in each area (1-2 sentences). The more you over describe or over express the least likely you are to get your objective met.

LOOK FOR

an example at www.herruck.com

HER RUCK

If your Relationship is your top priority, than use the GIVE skill.

G   be **GENTLE** in your approach. Be nice. No attacks, no threats, no judging, no eye rolling. Use a soft kind tone.

I   act **Interested**. Listen and appear interested in the other person's point of view. Face the person, use eye contact, and do not interrupt.

V   **Validate** with words and actions. Show that you understand the other person's feelings and thoughts about the situation.

E   Use an **Easy Manner**. Use a little humor, smile, and ease the person along the way. Be light-hearted; use a soft sell over a hard sell.

Remember to still follow the DEARMAN suggestions for getting the objective met, but utilize the GIVE technique versus the matter of fact tone of only using DEARMAN.

LOOK FOR

an example at www.herruck.com

HER RUCK

WHAT TO DO WHEN YOUR SELF-RESPECT IS # 1

If your Self-Respect is your top priority, than use the FAST skill.

(F) be **FAIR** to yourself and to the other person. Remember to validate your own feelings and wishes as well as the other person's.

(A) no **Apologies** for being alive, or making a request at all, for having an opinion, for disagreeing. No looking ashamed, with eyes and head down or body slumped. No invalidating the valid.

(S) Stick to **YOUR OWN** values. Don't sell out your values or integrity for reasons that aren't VERY important. Be clear on what you believe is the moral or valued way of thinking and acting. "Stick to your guns."

(T) **Be Truthful**. Don't lie or act helpless when you are not. Don't exaggerate or make up excuses.

Remember to still follow the DEARMAN suggestions for getting the objective met, but utilize the FAST technique versus the gentle manner of the GIVE skill.

LOOK FOR
an example at www.herruck.com

HER RUCK

"Your genetics loads the gun, your lifestyle pulls the trigger" –Mehmet Oz

I think we can agree, that our 'Rucks' are pretty full at times. There are many things out of our control (like our duty station) but there are lots of things within our control. We can control how we respond and rebound from stress.

One of the ways we can do this is by learning to reduce our vulnerability to our emotion mind with the **ABC PLEASE** skill.

A = Accumulating Positive Emotions

Short term: Do pleasant things that are possible now.
* Do one thing each day that leads to positive emotions
* Avoid avoiding
* Be mindful of pleasant events
* Be unmindful of worries

Long term: Make changes in your life so that positive events will happen more often in the future.

1. Avoid Avoiding (start now) 2. Identify values that are important to you ie: be productive, be part of a group, treat others well, be physically fit 3. Identify one value to work on now. 4. Identify a few goals related to this value (Be specific) 5. Choose one goal to work on now. 6. Identify small action steps toward your goal. 7. Take one action step now.

LEARN MORE ABOUT
this skill on our website at www.herruck.com

HER RUCK

PLEASANT EVENTS LIST

- [ ] Working on my car
- [ ] Planning a career
- [ ] Getting out of debt
- [ ] Collecting things
- [ ] Going on vacation
- [ ] Thinking how it will be when I finish school
- [ ] Recycling old items
- [ ] Going on a date
- [ ] Going to or watching a movie
- [ ] Jogging, walking
- [ ] Thinking "I have done a full day's work"
- [ ] Listening to music
- [ ] Thinking about past parties
- [ ] Buying household gadgets
- [ ] Lying in the sun
- [ ] Planning a career change
- [ ] Laughing
- [ ] Thinking about past trips
- [ ] Listening to other people
- [ ] Reading magazines
- [ ] Engaging in hobbies
- [ ] Spending an evening with friends

- [ ] Having a quiet evening
- [ ] Taking care of my plants
- [ ] Going swimming
- [ ] Going to a spa
- [ ] Getting your hair done
- [ ] Doodling/Drawing
- [ ] Exercising
- [ ] Playing Golf
- [ ] Going bowling
- [ ] Flying kites
- [ ] Having a family get together
- [ ] Riding a bike
- [ ] Going camping
- [ ] Singing around the house
- [ ] Arranging flowers
- [ ] Going to church
- [ ] Going to the beach
- [ ] Going sailing
- [ ] Travelling
- [ ] Painting
- [ ] Doing something spontaneously
- [ ] Driving
- [ ] Entertaining
- [ ] Reading a new book

SHARE YOUR IDEAS WITH THE GROUP
or if completing individually
check out more ideas at www.herruck.com

HER RUCK

B = Building Mastery

You build mastery when you do things that make you feel competent and effective. You build self-respect when you are confident in your abilities. Overcoming obstacles is one route to mastery. Most successful people in this world do not have fewer obstacles; they just get up after falling down. Mastery is achieved when you do things activities that make you feel competent, confident, in control, in areas that you would be willing to be challenged. Think of dance or piano recitals. A person must learn and build their competency first. Then they would be confident enough to face an audience and up to the challenge of the performance.

Steps to build mastery

1. Plan on doing at least one thing each day to build a sense of accomplishment:

2. Plan for success, not failure. Do something difficult, but possible.

3. Gradually increase the difficulty over time. If the first task is too difficult, do something a little easier next time.

4. Look for a challenge. If the task is too easy, try something a little harder next time.

LEARN MORE ABOUT
this skill on our website at www.herruck.com

HER RUCK

IDEAS FOR BUILDING MASTERY

Create a list of areas you would like to build mastery.

....

....

....

....

....

....

Pick one to work on now and list the steps it will take to accomplish this goal.

....

....

....

....

....

....

SHARE YOURS WITH THE GROUP OR
check out our list at www.herruck.com

HER RUCK

C = Cope Ahead of Time with Difficult Situation

Coping ahead is mindful as it is the intentional focus on planning for the foreseeable future. If you are possibly falling down on PCS orders but they haven't officially came through yet, it is a good idea to create a plan for coping with the stress ahead of time. You will be more likely to make a wise mind tentative plan before the emotions of the actual event are stronger. (Other difficult situations could include loss of pet, loss of job, ending friendships, death of grandparent, etc)

Steps to Cope Ahead

1. Describe the situation that is likely to occur or prompt a problem behavior: check the facts. Name the emotions and actions likely to interfere with your wise mind.

2. Decide what coping or problem-solving techniques you want to use in the situation. Be specific. Write out in detail how you will cope with the situation with your emotions.

3. Imagine the situation in your mind as vividly as possible. Imagine yourself in the situation now, not watching the situation.

4. Rehearse in your mind coping effectively. Practice in your mind what you can do, what you can think, what you can say, and how you can say it. Rehearse coping effectively with new problems that come up including your most feared catastrophe.

5. Practice **RELAXATION** after rehearsing.

HER RUCK

Take care of your mind by taking care of your body

(PL) Treat Physical Illness. Take care of your body and see a doctor when necessary. Take prescribed medications or alternatives consistently.

(E) Balanced Eating. Don't eat too much or too little. Eat regularly and mindfully. Stay away from foods that make you feel emotional.

(A) Avoid Mood-Altering Substances. Stay off illicit drugs, and use alcohol in moderation (if at all).

(S) Balance Sleep. Try to get 7-9 hours of sleep a night, or at least the amount of sleep that helps you feel good. Seek advice if you are having difficulty maintaining a sleep schedule.

(E) Get Exercise. Do some sort of exercise every day. Try to build up to 20 minutes of daily exercise.

LEARN MORE ABOUT
this skill on our website at www.herruck.com

HER RUCK

Emotions serve a purpose. They communicate to others, motivate action, and are self validating. A common complaint in relationships is that one member may over express their emotions or under express emotions. To increase relationships and getting your needs met, it is important to accurately identify and express emotions.

Many emotions and actions are set off by our thoughts and interpretations of events not by the events themselves.

Changing your beliefs and assumptions to fit the facts can help you change your emotional reactions to situations.

To check whether your emotional reactions fit the facts of the situation it is good to Check the Facts.

Check the Facts by:

1. Ask: What is the emotion I want to change?

2. Ask: What is the event prompting my emotion?

3. Ask: What are my interpretations, thoughts, and assumptions about the event? Practice looking at all sides of the situation.

4. Ask: Am I assuming a threat? Label the threat. Assess the probability that the threatening event will really occur.

5. Ask: What's the catastrophe? Imagine the catastrophe really occurring. Imagine coping well with a catastrophe.

6. Ask: Does my emotion and/or its intensity fit the actual facts?

LEARN MORE ABOUT
on our website at www.herruck.com

EMOTIONS THAT FIT THE FACTS

FEAR:
1. There is a threat to your life or that of someone you care about.
2. There is a threat to your health or that of someone you care about.
3. There is a threat to your well-being or that of someone you care about.

ANGER:
1. An important goal is blocked or a desired activity is interrupted or prevented.
2. You or someone you care about is attacked or hurt by others.
3. You or someone you care about is insulted or threatened by others.
4. The integrity or status of your social group is offended or threatened.

ENVY:
1. Another person or group gets or has things you don't have that you want or need.

JEALOUSY:
1. A very important and desired relationship or object in your life is in danger of being damaged or lost.
2. Someone is threatening to take a valued relationship or object away from you.

SADNESS:
1. You have lost something or someone permanently.
2. Things are not the way you wanted or expected and hoped them to be.

GUILT:
1. Your own behavior violates your moral code.

Intensity and duration of an emotion are justified by:
1. How likely it is that the expected outcomes will occur.
2. How great and/or important the outcomes are.
3. how effective the emotion is in your life now.

emotions on our website at www.herruck.com

HER RUCK

The ability to tolerate stress is important as a military spouse. We need to be able to survive a crisis situation without making things worse, and accept reality as it is.

You are in a crisis when the situation is:

1. Highly Stressful
2. Short-term (that is it won't last a long time)
3. Creates intense pressure to resolve the crisis now.

Use Crisis Survival Skills when:

1. You have intense pain that cannot be helped quickly
2. You want to act on your emotions, but it will only make things worse.
3. Emotion mind threatens to overwhelm you, and you need to stay skilful.
4. You are overwhelmed, yet demands must be met.
5. Arousal is extreme, but problems can't be solved immediately.

Don't Use Crisis Survival Skills for:

* Everyday problems
* Solving all your life problems
* Making your life worth living or more valuable

LEARN MORE

crisis survival skills on our website at www.herruck.com

HER RUCK

Stop	Do not just react! Stop! Freeze! Do not move a muscle! Your emotions may try to make you act without thinking. Stay in control.
Take a step back	Take a step back from the situation. Take a long break. Let go. Take a deep breath. Do not let your feelings make you act impulsively.
Observe	Notice what is going on inside and outside you. What is the situation? What are your thoughts and feelings? What are others saying or doing?
Proceed Mindfully	Act with awareness. In deciding what to do, consider your thoughts and feelings, the situation, and other people's thoughts and feelings. Think about your goals. Ask Wise Mind: Which action will make it better or worse.

LEARN MORE

crisis survival skills on our website at www.herruck.com

HER RUCK

WHEN THE CRISIS IS ADDICTION

Addictions are a real issue for many military spouses. You are addicted when you are unable to stop a behavior pattern or use of substances, despite negative consequences and despite your best efforts to stop. If you think you have no addictions, check out this list.

* Alcohol * Attention Seeking * Avoiding _____ *Auto racing
* Betting * Bulimia * Cheating * Coffee * Collecting (art, coins, junk, clothes, shoes, etc) *Computers * Criminal activities *Dieting *Drugs *Diuretics *E-mail
* Food/eating *Gambling *Games/puzzles *Gossiping *Imagining/fantasizing
* Internet *Internet games *Shoplifting/stealing * Lying *Pornography * Reckless driving * Risky behaviors *Self-inflicted injury *Sex *Shopping
* Sleeping *Smartphone apps *Smoking/Tobacco *Social Networking * Soda
* Speed * Spiritual Practices *Sports/Activities *Television *Texting
* Vandalism * Videos *Video games *Working

Skills to Learn When Dealing with Addiction DCBA

Dialectical Abstinence Clear Mind &
Community Reinforcement Burning
Bridges & Building New Ones
Alternate Rebellion & Adaptive Denial

LEARN THESE
addiction skills on our website at www.herruck.com

HER RUCK

It is a fact of life that problems will occur.

There are 4 options when dealing with a problem

1. Solve the problem
2. Feel Better about the problem
3. Tolerate the problem
4. Stay Miserable

Consider using a notebook piece of paper and trying the 5 steps to problem solving on a current problem.

5 Steps to Problem Solving

1. DESCRIBE the details of your problem. Focus on the facts.
2. BRAINSTORM ideas for solving your problem. List as many creative ideas as possible, without judging your ideas.
3. List the PROS & CONS of your favorite ideas.
4. MAKE A CHOICE & TAKE ACTION. Participate Mindfully in solving your problem.
5. EVALUATE your Outcomes

LEARN MORE ABOUT
Problem Solving on our website at www.herruck.com

HER RUCK

IDEAS FOR BUILDING MASTERY

Create a list of area's you would like to build mastery.

....

....

....

....

....

....

Pick one to work on now and list the steps it will take to accomplish this goal.

....

....

....

....

....

....

....

....

SHARE YOURS WITH THE GROUP OR
check out our list at www.herruck.com

HER RUCK

BARRIERS THAT GET IN THE WAY

Sometimes no matter how skillful we want to be, we still have things that get in the way. Identifying your barriers can help you overcome them. Here is a short list of some of the barriers that could be getting in the way.

LACK OF SKILL

You actually don't know what to say or how to act. You don't know what will work.

WORRY THOUGHTS

You have the ability, but your worrying thoughts are getting in the way.

BIOLOGY

Biological factors can make emotions or actions harder. You may not have the physical capabilities.

ENVIRONMENT

This is prevalent in the military lifestyle. No matter how skillful you are, the environment makes it impossible for you to be effective. Sometimes other people have the power and control.

EMOTIONS

Your emotions get in the way of you acting effectively. Your current mood controls you. You don't want to put in the effort, or are incapable because of intense emotions.

at www.herruck.com

HER RUCK

AFFIRMATIONS

Create a list of your favorite Cheerleading statements/ motivational quotes or prayers that help you when you are having a hard time (feel free to glue in pictures).

....

....

....

....

....

....

....

....

....

....

....

....

....

....

....

....

....

....

NEED INSPIRATION?

Check out our website at www.herruck.com

HER RUCK

Journaling focuses on your internal experiences, thoughts and feelings. Journaling uses reflective writing so that you can receive mental and emotional clarity, validate experiences and come to a deeper understanding of yourself.

Some people free write in journals while others prefers journal prompts. In the next few pages, there will be journal prompts followed by blank pages for free writing. Journaling is a great habit to start and a great routine for your mornings or evenings. It is a way to take time for yourself.

Journal Prompt 1: **I couldn't imagine my life without...**

....

....

....

....

....

....

....

....

....

....

Journal Prompt 2: **When I'm in pain (physical or emotional) the kindest thing I can do for myself is…**

....

....

....

....

....

....

....

....

....

....

....

....

....

....

....

....

....

....

Journal Prompt 3: I really wish others knew this about me...

Journal Prompt 4: Name a compassionate way you've supported a friend recently. Then write down how you can do the same for yourself.

Journal Prompt 5: Make a list of the people in your life who genuinely support you, and who you can genuinely trust.

Journal Prompt 6: What always brings tears to your eyes?

Journal Prompt 7: **Using 10 words, describe yourself.**

Journal Prompt 8: **What's surprised you the most about your life or life in general?**

....

....

....

....

....

....

....

....

....

....

....

....

....

....

....

....

....

....

....

....

Journal Prompt 9: **Write a list of questions to which you urgently need answers.**

Journal Prompt 10: **Write the words you need to hear (from your spouse, your parents, your kids, yourself)**

HER RUCK

Personal Reflections contd...

Personal Reflections contd...

Personal Reflections contd...

Personal Reflections contd...

Made in the USA
Columbia, SC
01 October 2020